World *Cities*

BERLIN

Christine Hatt

Belitha Press

First published in the UK in 1999 by

Belitha Press Limited
London House, Great Eastern Wharf,
Parkgate Road, London SW11 4NQ

Copyright © Belitha Press Ltd 1999
Text copyright © Christine Hatt 1999

ISBN 1 84138 043 1

British Library Cataloguing in Publication Data for
this book is available from the British Library.

Printed in Singapore

Editor Stephanie Bellwood
Designer Hayley Cove
Map illustrator Lorraine Harrison
Picture researcher Kathy Lockley
Consultant Carl Wade
Educational consultant Elizabeth Lewis
Picture acknowledgements
AKG London: 8, 9t, 9b, 10t, 10b, 11b, 11t, 12b, 14t, 15b, 18b, 19b, 21t,
21b, 22t, 22b, 23t, 24, 27b, 30t, 33, 34b, 36t, 36b, 37t, 39t, 40l, 40r, 41b,
41t, 42t, 42b, Cover b; Anthony Blake Photo Library: 32t; Britstock-Ifa:
1, 4, 5t, 5b, 16, 17t, 17b, 19t, 20b, 20t, 25t, 28b, 28t, 29t, 30b, 35t, 35b,
37b, 39b, 43cl, 43c, Cover tl; Robert Harding Picture Library: 34t; Helga
Lade Fotoagentur: 26t; PowerStock/Zefa: 14b, 15tr, 25b, Cover tr; Rex
Features: 12b, 12t, 18t, 26b, 27t, 29b, 31b, 31t, 38t, 43b; Frank Spooner
Pictures: 23b, 38b; TRIP: 12t, 32b.

Words in **bold** are explained in the glossary on pages 46 and 47.

CONTENTS

Berlin is the capital of the **Federal** Republic of Germany. It stands in the north-east of the country on the banks of the River Spree. Berlin is the largest city in Germany, with an area of about 889 square kilometres and a population of just under three and a half million. The Berlin region, also known as Greater Berlin, extends beyond the city borders and contains about one million more people.

Division and unity

In 1949 Germany and the city of Berlin were divided into two parts – the **Communist** East and the **capitalist** West. Both city and country were joined again in 1990, and since then there have been many changes. In Berlin the authorities are working hard to create a fully united city, for example by linking the transport networks of the East and the West.

▲ This view of Berlin shows the Brandenburg Gate (right of the semi-circle of trees) and the Reichstag (above the trees by the river).

BERLIN

STATUS
Capital of the Federal Republic of Germany;
one of the country's 16 *Länder*

AREA
889 square kilometres

POPULATION
3.47 million (1996)

GOVERNING BODY
Land government and mayor;
borough assemblies and mayors

CLIMATE
Temperatures average -1°C in January
and 18°C in July

TIME ZONE
Greenwich Mean Time plus one hour

CURRENCY
1 Deutschmark (DM) = 100 pfennigs
(The Euro will fully replace the DM by July 2002)

OFFICIAL LANGUAGE
German

Land and local government

Berlin is a ***Land***, one of the 16 federal **states** that make up Germany. It has a state parliament and government, led by a mayor. Each of Berlin's 23 boroughs also elects its own mayor and **assembly**. Together they form the city's local government.

◄ This building is the Red Town Hall (Rotes Rathaus), where Berlin's mayor works. It used to be the home of the East Berlin government.

Berlin and Brandenburg

The government of Berlin may change, as there is a plan to join the *Land* of Berlin with the nearby *Land* of Brandenburg. People voted against this in 1996, but a new vote is likely soon. The number of boroughs may be cut down, too, to make local government simpler.

Capital city

East Berlin was the capital of East Germany under Communist rule. West Germany was ruled from the city of Bonn. Berlin became the capital of the whole country again in 1991, and German politicians voted to move back there. Parliament relocates to Berlin in 1999 (see page 42).

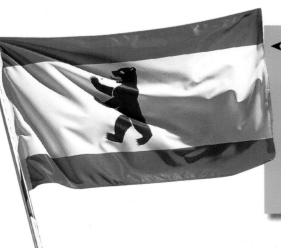

◄ Long ago people hunted bears in the woods around Berlin. Now the bear is the symbol of the city and appears on its flag.

MAPS OF THE CITY

 The main map on this page shows you Berlin as it looks today. Many of the sites mentioned in the book are marked and some are illustrated.

The smaller map shows the city's 23 boroughs. It will help you to locate some of the places mentioned on other pages.

BERLIN'S BOROUGHS

see map of
central Berlin

1	Reinickendorf	**13**	Spandau
2	Pankow	**14**	Zehlendorf
3	Weissensee	**15**	Steglitz
4	Wedding	**16**	Tempelhof
5	Prenzlauer Berg	**17**	Neukölln
6	Tiergarten	**18**	Treptow
7	Mitte	**19**	Köpenick
8	Friedrichshain	**20**	Hellersdorf
9	Kreuzberg	**21**	Marzahn
10	Schöneberg	**22**	Lichtenberg
11	Wilmersdorf	**23**	Hohenschönhausen
12	Charlottenburg		

CENTRAL BERLIN

RIVER SPREE

LANDWEH CANAL

1. Kurfürstendamm
2. Kaiser William Memorial Church
3. New church and tower
4. Europa-Center
5. Tiergarten
6. Victory Column
7. Kulturforum
8. Philharmonie
9. Sony Centre
10. Daimler-Benz area
11. Potsdamer Platz
12. Holocaust memorial site
13. Brandenburg Gate
14. Reichstag
15. German Theatre
16. Berliner Ensemble
17. Haus am Checkpoint Charlie
18. French Cathedral
19. Konzerthaus
20. German Cathedral
21. Gendarmenmarkt
22. State Opera House
23. Humboldt University
24. New Synagogue
25. Bode Museum
26. Pergamon Museum
27. Old National Gallery
28. Old Museum
29. St Marien Church
30. Television Tower
31. Red Town Hall
32. St Nicholas Church
33. Alexanderplatz

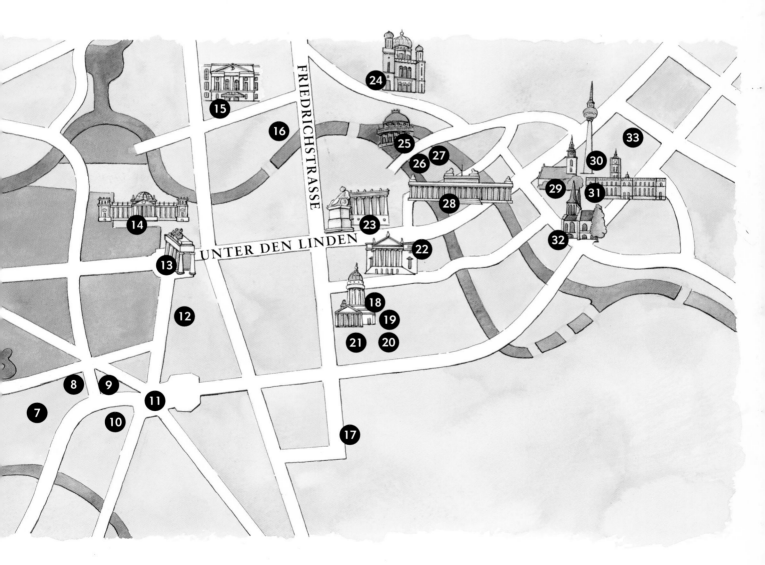

In the early 13th century two trading settlements, Cölln and Berlin, were founded on the site of modern Berlin. Cölln, which was first mentioned in written records in 1237, stood on an island in the River Spree. Berlin, first mentioned in 1244, stood on the north bank opposite. In 1307 the two towns were united.

The Hohenzollern family

Berlin-Cölln was part of the Brandenburg region. From the 15th century it was ruled by princes of the Hohenzollern family. These princes took over Berlin-Cölln, built a palace and made the city their capital. Between 1618 and 1648 Protestants and Roman Catholics from many European countries opposed each other in the Thirty Years' War. Fighting raged in Berlin-Cölln and disease also swept through the city. About half of its 12,000 inhabitants had died by the end of this period.

Powerful rulers

In 1640 a new ruler took over in Brandenburg. This was Frederick William, known as the Great **Elector**. He built **fortifications**, canals and houses in Berlin-Cölln, and brought about 6,000 **Huguenots** (French Protestants) to the city to replace inhabitants killed in the war. When Frederick William died in 1688, his son Frederick became Elector, and in 1701 was crowned King Frederick I. He controlled the territory of **Prussia**, an area which included Brandenburg. In 1709 the king united Berlin, Cölln and three nearby towns to form the single city of Berlin.

◄ Huguenots came to Berlin after their religion was banned in France in 1685. This imaginative picture shows the Great Elector welcoming them.

Frederick the Great increased the size ➤ of Prussia's army. It became Europe's largest, with 180,000 members.

Frederick the Great

King Frederick II began his reign in 1740. He made Prussia a great military power, and it became the most important **state** in northern Germany. Frederick also ordered the construction of many grand Berlin buildings, even though he preferred to live in Sanssouci Palace in nearby Potsdam. He is known as Frederick the Great because of his achievements.

19th-century Berlin

In 1806 the armies of **Napoleon Bonaparte** occupied Berlin and stayed until 1808. In the following years workers in the many new factories called for better pay and conditions. People also began to demand a **constitution** and a parliament for the city. In 1848 there was a revolution, and from 1849 the king had to rule with a parliament.

The German Empire

On 18 January 1871 Prussia joined the other German states to form the German Empire. The Prussian king William I became Kaiser (Emperor) with Otto von Bismarck, the Prussian prime minister, as Chancellor. The Prussian city of Berlin became the **imperial** capital.

◀ William I was proclaimed German Emperor in the Hall of Mirrors at the Palace of Versailles, near Paris, France. This painting shows the dramatic scene.

In the **First World War** (1914-18) Germany fought many countries, including Britain, France, Russia and the USA. A total of about ten million people died. Germany was defeated, and Kaiser William II **abdicated**.

The Weimar Republic

The German Empire was replaced by a **republic**. In 1919 a Social Democrat government was formed in the town of Weimar. But Berlin was still Germany's capital and in 1920 expanded to form Greater Berlin. **Inflation** and unemployment grew quickly in Germany. Many people turned to the **Nazi Party** for help. On 30 January 1933 its leader, Adolf Hitler, became German Chancellor. He ended the Weimar Republic and began a period of **Nazi** rule called the Third Reich.

Chancellor Adolf Hitler (left) ▼ with German President Paul von Hindenburg in 1933. When Hindenburg died in 1934 Hitler took on both roles and named himself **Führer**.

The Second World War

The Nazis **persecuted** Germany's Jews and anyone who disagreed with Nazi policies. Then, on 1 September 1939, they invaded Poland and the **Second World War** broke out. Much of Berlin was destroyed by the **Allies** in **air raids**, and up to 50,000 citizens were killed. In January 1945 **Soviet** troops invaded Germany. By April they were in Berlin. Hitler committed suicide, and Germany surrendered on 8 May.

◄ Second World War bombing left about 100 million tonnes of rubble on Berlin's streets. Many men were dead or in prison camps, so 'rubble women' cleared away the debris.

During the Berlin Airlift cargo ➤ planes brought thousands of tonnes of supplies into the city every day, including chocolate and sweets.

The Berlin Airlift

After the war the four main Allies **occupied** Germany. Each controlled a separate zone. Berlin was in the eastern, Soviet zone, and was itself divided between the four Allies. The Soviet sector was in the east. Soon the **Communist** Soviets and the other, non-Communist Allies came into conflict. In June 1948 the Soviets closed all road, rail and canal links between West Germany and West Berlin. Supplies could not get through, so the other Allies had to airlift food and fuel into West Berlin. The blockade ended in May 1949.

East and West Germany

In May 1949 the British, French and American zones formed the **Federal** Republic of Germany (West Germany), with Bonn as its capital. In October the Soviet zone became the German Democratic Republic (East Germany), with East Berlin as its capital. East Berlin was poorer than West Berlin, so many people fled to the West. The East German government erected the Berlin Wall in 1961 to prevent more escapes. This wire and concrete barrier ran right through the city.

The fall of the Berlin Wall ▼ symbolized the end of the **Cold War** and the hope of a new future.

Together again

In the 1980s East Germans protested against the lack of **democracy** in their country. This led to the collapse of the government. Germans began to break down the Berlin Wall on 9 November 1989. On 3 October 1990 East and West Germany were reunited, and in 1991 Berlin became the capital of the whole country again.

THE PEOPLE OF BERLIN

 When Berlin was reunited in 1990 people were overjoyed. But the 2.2 million West Berliners and 1.3 million East Berliners are starting to realize the cost of what they call *die Wende* ('the change'). As a result there is often tension between the two groups.

Berliners soon discovered that ▲ **reunification** had disadvantages. 'We want jobs not pay-offs' is one of the slogans used in this protest.

East and West Berliners

Under **Communist** rule, many East Berliners had guaranteed jobs and financial help from the government to pay their rent. Now they have lost these benefits, and a third are unemployed. They are also angry because rich West Berliners are moving in to build new, expensive houses. This has driven up prices and forced East Berliners out. West Berliners are complaining too because they have to pay high taxes to fund the reconstruction of run-down East Berlin.

NEO-NAZISM

Berlin's economic difficulties have led to the growth of neo-Nazism (new Nazism) in the city. Many neo-**Nazis** are unemployed young men from eastern boroughs such as Marzahn and Lichtenberg. They dress as skinheads (right) and sometimes carry out violent attacks on **immigrants**. They are also suspected of attacks on Jewish cemeteries and memorials.

World Cities 🌐 12

New arrivals

Just over 12 per cent of Berliners are not Germans. Turks make up the city's largest non-German population – about a third of the total. Most came to the city after the Berlin Wall went up in 1961. At that time businesses in West Berlin could not employ East Berliners, so they used guest workers (*Gastarbeiter*). Most Turkish workers settled in the borough of Kreuzberg, where many still live. Since 1990 people from Poland and the former USSR have arrived, as well as war refugees from the former Yugoslavia.

This grocery shop has signs in Arabic and ▲ German. Different nationalities in Berlin have introduced new foods (see page 32).

▲ Berliners gaze in disbelief at the debris of a Jewish shop after *Kristallnacht*. Behind is the swastika, emblem of the Nazi party.

Berlin's Jews

Jews have lived in Berlin for hundreds of years. In the 17th century Jewish victims of **pogroms** in Russia and Eastern Europe fled to Berlin. By the 1930s about 170,000 lived in the city. When the Nazis came to power in 1933, Jews were sacked from their jobs and banned from mixing with non-Jews. Then, on 9 November 1938, the Nazis launched an all-out attack, destroying Jewish shops and **synagogues**. This is known as *Kristallnacht* ('crystal night') because of all the broken glass in the streets.

Loss and renewal

Many Jews left Germany during the Nazi era. Millions more died in **concentration camps**. By the end of the **Second World War** only about 5,000 Jews remained in Berlin. Since then they have slowly returned. The city's present Jewish population of about 10,500 is the largest in Germany. Many Jews live in the old Jewish district on the north bank of the River Spree.

Many gifted architects have worked in Berlin. As a result there are hundreds of splendid buildings in the city.

GERMANIA

Nazi leader Adolf Hitler wanted to rebuild Berlin completely. He intended to call his new capital Germania and to fill it with huge buildings that reflected Germany's power. Architect Albert Speer completed the first of these buildings in 1938 – the Chancellery (above) where Hitler worked. The Nazis' defeat in the Second World War ended their dreams of Berlin's reconstruction; and the Chancellery was pulled down by the **Soviet** army.

Charlottenburg Castle was first ➤ called Lutzenburg Castle. It was renamed by Frederick I after his wife, Sophie-Charlotte.

St Nicholas Church

Berlin's oldest district is the St Nicholas Quarter (Nikolaiviertel), and the oldest building there is St Nicholas Church (Nikolaikirche). The church was built in about 1230, but was badly damaged in the **Second World War**. Much of the quarter, including St Nicholas Church, was restored in 1987 for Berlin's 750th anniversary celebrations. The church is now a museum of Berlin history.

Charlottenburg Castle

The beautiful Charlottenburg Castle (Schloss Charlottenburg) was built in the late 17th century as a summer home for Sophie-Charlotte, wife of King Frederick I (see page 8). Many architects, including Karl Friedrich Schinkel (see page 40), extended the building and it is now about five times its original size. The chapel and some royal apartments are open to the public. The castle also contains museums and galleries.

The Brandenburg Gate

The Brandenburg Gate is one of Berlin's greatest monuments. It stands at the western end of Berlin's grandest avenue, Unter den Linden, and it formed part of the border between East and West when the city was divided. The stone archway was designed by architect Carl Gotthard Langhans and was completed in 1791. The copper statue on the top is a chariot drawn by four horses and driven by a woman who represents Victory. It is known as the *Quadriga*.

When **Napoleon Bonaparte** occupied ▲ Berlin (see page 9), he sent the *Quadriga* to France. It was returned to Berlin in 1814.

▲ Berliners call the ruins of the Kaiser William Memorial Church 'the broken tooth' and its streamlined modern neighbour 'the lipstick'.

The Reichstag

This grand, domed building housed the parliament of the German Empire from 1894. The Reichstag was damaged by fire in 1933 and by shrapnel in the Second World War, but it survived. The building is now being restored (see page 42), and from 1999 the German parliament will be based there again.

Kaiser William Memorial Church

The Kaiser William Memorial Church (Kaiser-Wilhelm-Gedächtniskirche) was built in 1895 as a tribute to Kaiser William I. In the Second World War it was almost destroyed, and it has been left to stand in ruins as a reminder of the horrors of war. A new church stands next to it as a sign of hope.

OPEN SPACES

Berlin is a green city. Almost a quarter of its area is covered in pine and other woods, while trees line many of its streets. It contains many parks, too, as well as lakes and beaches a short distance from the centre.

The 67m-high Victory Column ▼ towers over the Great Star roundabout in the Tiergarten. A golden statue of a winged woman stands on the top.

The Tiergarten

Berlin's largest park is the Tiergarten. It extends for about three kilometres from east to west. The site was originally a forest, but Frederick the Great turned it into a landscaped garden. Berliners now enjoy its green spaces. The park contains several fascinating buildings such as Bellevue Castle (Schloss Bellevue), and the Victory Column (Siegessäule), which commemorates **Prussia**'s 19th-century war successes. There is also a zoo and an aquarium.

The Grunewald

The Grunewald is a huge, dense forest on Berlin's western edge. It contains about 25 million trees and is the home of deer, rabbits and other wildlife. Many Berliners go there for picnics or to walk or cycle along its woodland paths. Special features of the Grunewald include the 'Devil's Mountain' (Teufelsberg). This 115m-high hill was built from **Second World War** rubble. People ski down its snow-covered slopes in winter.

Wannsee

South of the Grunewald is another famous outdoor spot called Wannsee. This resort stands on the edge of a lake formed by the River Havel. The lake is rimmed with a kilometre of sand, the longest inland beach in Europe. In warm weather crowds of Berliners arrive to enjoy the sun or swim in the water close to the shore. Boats travel to and fro further out, some towing water-skiers behind them.

At Wannsee people keep their ▲ belongings in small wicker shelters. They are not allowed to play radios that disturb the peace of the area.

Peacock Island

The 98-hectare Peacock Island (Pfaueninsel) lies in the River Havel, to the south of Wannsee. In 1793 it was bought by the Prussian king Frederick William II, who built a small castle there. Visitors can still see it today. Later royal residents created beautiful gardens on the island and brought many animals there. Most of these are now in Tiergarten Zoo, but the peacocks after whom the island is named still strut around its land.

▲ A wary bird stands in front of the castle on Peacock Island. Builders deliberately made the castle look like a romantic ruin.

GARDENING

Many Berliners are keen gardeners. About 80,000 small gardens (Kleingarten) cover 6,000 hectares of the city. These gardens are not attached to houses, but each has its own summer hut alongside. The garden-owners often join their gardens together to form 'colonies'. All the colony members can wander freely from one garden to the next, along a corridor of greenery.

HOMES AND HOUSING

Over the years the Berlin authorities have devised many plans to provide homes for all Berliners, yet the city has a serious housing shortage.

Tenement blocks

In 1862 a new layout was prepared for the city of Berlin. It led to the construction of thousands of **tenement** blocks grouped around courtyards. These homes were needed for Berlin's growing population of factory workers. Although the blocks were beautifully decorated on the outside, the flats inside were often dark and overcrowded. Some of these blocks still stand and many are being renovated to make comfortable homes.

Restoration work in the city of ▲ Berlin has transformed one of these tenement blocks (right), but the other is crumbling away.

The buildings that make up the Uncle ▼ Tom's Cabin estate are all different colours and styles. About 15,000 people live there.

Housing estates

In the 1920s another house-building phase began in Berlin. Famous architects such as Walter Gropius were employed to design decent housing estates for poor families. These estates consisted of blocks of flats and were often built near woods or other green spaces. Many, such as the Uncle Tom's Cabin estate in the south-western borough of Zehlendorf, are still home to Berliners today.

In the 1970s a **Communist** new town called Marzahn was built in East Berlin. It had many grey concrete tower blocks.

EXHIBITIONS

There have been several architectural exhibitions in Berlin. Architects who attended built all kinds of homes in the capital. For example the Hansa Quarter (Hansaviertel) near the Tiergarten was built for an exhibition in 1957. Its houses were designed by 53 architects from around the world. For a 1987 exhibition architects constructed new homes and renovated old tenements, particularly for **immigrants** in boroughs such as Kreuzberg.

The Second World War and after

Nearly half of Berlin's flats were destroyed in the **Second World War**, so major building work began in the post-war years. After the city was divided, East and West Berlin developed separately. In the 1960s and 1970s large housing estates were built on both sides. In the East most were made of grey **prefabricated** concrete. In the West designs were more varied and colourful.

Courtyard buildings in the Hackescher ▲ Markt area have now been renovated and contain homes, theatres, galleries and cafés.

The squatter movement

In the 1960s many West Berliners, especially students, protested against the high cost of housing. Hundreds moved into derelict flats in boroughs such as Kreuzberg and turned them into **squats**. For a long time the city authorities did not stop them, as the squatters often improved the buildings. But in the 1980s the squats were cleared by police. This led to riots, but the squatter movement never recovered.

Housing today

Since **reunification** many people have moved to Berlin. More will follow when the parliament arrives in 1999. As a result the city will need thousands of new homes by the year 2000. Many construction programmes are under way to provide them. Builders are also renovating old flats, especially in the former East Berlin, for example in the Hackescher Markt area.

EDUCATION

All German children have a right to a **kindergarten** place, but they do not have to attend. They must start full-time schooling at the age of six and continue their education for twelve years. They may leave secondary school after completing ten years of study, but only if they go on to a **vocational** school to train for a career.

▲ A German primary school class. Berlin children stay at primary school for two years longer than those in other *Länder*.

Berlin schools

Berlin children stay at primary school for six years. They then attend one of several types of secondary school, such as a high school or comprehensive. There are many vocational schools for older children. Before **reunification** many vocational schools in East Berlin were linked to factories. Now they are independent and most specialize in a particular field, such as electronics or hairdressing.

Berlin universities

Berlin has three universities. The oldest was founded in 1810 by Wilhelm von Humboldt and later named after him. Karl Marx, the founder of Communism, was a student there. Humboldt University lies in the former East Berlin. Its lecturers were not allowed to express their ideas freely during the Communist era, so in 1948 some moved to West Berlin and established the Free University. Its students played a big part in the protests that swept the city in the 1960s (see page 19). Berlin's third university is the Technical University, founded in 1879. It teaches a range of science subjects.

Members of the ▲
Technical University
and the Fraunhofer
Society, a research
organization, work in
this building. They
devise new machines
and robots here.

Specialist colleges

Berlin has many other centres of higher education known as 'subject high schools' (Fachhochschulen). They provide specialist training for various careers. Among the most famous are the Hanns Eisler College of Music and the Bruno Leuschner College of Economics.

SCIENCE CENTRE

Berlin is Germany's major centre for scientific research. It first became important in 1910, when the Kaiser William Society for the Promotion of Sciences was set up there. During the 1920s some of the world's greatest scientists worked for the society, including Albert Einstein (right) and Max Planck. In 1948 the organization was renamed the Max Planck Society. There are many other centres of scientific study in the city. Builders are also constructing a huge research and technology park in the south-eastern suburb of Adlershof. About 30,000 researchers from universities and industries will work there.

◄ Standing outside
Humboldt University
is a statue of its
founder, Wilhelm
von Humboldt. There
is also this statue of
his brother Alexander,
a famous explorer.

In the 16th century the German priest Martin Luther began a movement to reform the Roman Catholic Church. This led to the setting up of Protestant churches. Over the years there was constant conflict between Catholics and Protestants, leading to the Thirty Years' War (see page 8). Today Catholics and Protestants live peacefully side by side in Berlin. Many Jews and Muslims also practise their religions in the city.

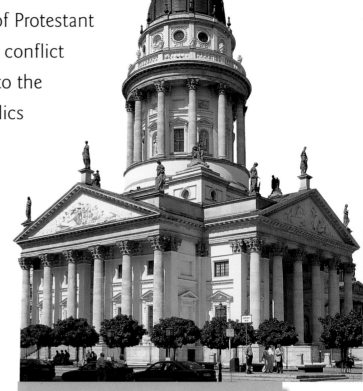

▲ The German Cathedral (above) and the French Cathedral stand at either end of Gendarmenmarkt Square.

THE ENLIGHTENMENT

In the 18th century a movement called the Enlightenment grew in Europe. Enlightenment thinkers believed in the importance of reason and science. Many also disapproved of religion, which they thought was just superstition.

Berlin was the centre of the movement in Germany. The city's leading Enlightenment figures were dramatist Gotthold Lessing and Jewish philosopher Moses Mendelssohn (above). The king, Frederick the Great (see page 9), encouraged the discussion of Enlightenment ideas at his palace in Potsdam.

Protestant churches

There are many Protestant churches in the city. Berlin Cathedral was completed in 1905 for Kaiser William II. Two other Protestant cathedrals stand in Berlin's Gendarmenmarkt Square. The French Cathedral was built in 1701 for **Huguenots** (see page 8). French Protestants still worship in the church. The German Cathedral was once a place of worship for German **Calvinists**. It now houses an exhibition of German history.

The spectacular domes of the ➤
New Synagogue were restored
to their former glory during
reconstruction work.

Roman Catholic churches

St Marien Church (Marienkirche) is a
Roman Catholic church that was built
in about 1270. It is still a place of worship,
unlike the slightly older St Nicholas
Church (see page 14). The largest Catholic
church in Berlin is St Hedwig's Cathedral.
It was built in 1747 after Frederick the
Great conquered **Silesia**, where many
Roman Catholics lived.

Berlin synagogues

Berlin's Jews built many **synagogues** in the city.
The grandest was the New Synagogue (Neue
Synagoge), completed in 1866. On *Kristallnacht*,
23 of Berlin's 29 synagogues were destroyed.
The New Synagogue survived, but the **Nazis**
turned it into a warehouse. In 1943 it was badly
damaged by bombs. Reconstruction work
began in the 1980s and in 1995 the building
re-opened as a museum and cultural centre.

▲ Many of the city's Muslims
worship in the Berlin Mosque.
This man, called the imam,
leads the prayers. The mosque
can be seen in the background.

Muslims in Berlin

Most of Berlin's 140,000 Turks are Muslims.
As a result there are now many mosques in
the city. The Moshee Islamic Community is
in the south-western borough of Wilmersdorf,
and services are held there every Friday.

INDUSTRY AND FINANCE

Berlin became a major industrial centre in the early 19th century. Since then financial collapse, war and the division of the city have caused huge problems for Berlin businesses. The **reunification** of East and West Germany in 1990 has also brought unemployment. But industries – and jobs – are slowly returning.

 ◄ This area is known as Siemens Town (Siemensstadt). The Siemens company owns the land and built factories, offices and a huge housing estate there for its employees.

Early industry

The centre of industry in early Berlin was a place called Charité, in the Mitte borough. It had huge foundries for melting and moulding iron, and the flames and smoke earned the area the nickname 'fire land'. In 1837 August Borsig set up a factory there to make railway locomotives. In 1847 Werner Siemens founded an electrical company nearby. Both businesses did well, as did textile and porcelain industries, among others.

BERLIN BANKS

Berlin is an important financial centre. About 150 banks, including the Berlin Bank and the Deutsche (German) Bank, have offices in the city. In 1994 the Berlin Banking Company was established. Its role is to support the economic recovery of the new capital. Berlin also has its own stock exchange. People can visit this building in the Charlottenburg borough to watch all the frantic financial activity.

The new Sony Centre on ➤
Potsdamer Platz will contain
seven buildings, including
Sony's European headquarters
and a film museum.

Collapse and renewal

In 1929 a financial crisis in the USA led to the collapse of a lot of Berlin businesses. Many factories were later destroyed in the **Second World War**. After 1945 industry developed separately in East and West Berlin. The West German government provided money for businesses to set up in West Berlin, but many companies preferred to be in more accessible West German cities. East Berlin became the industrial centre of East Germany, making steel, chemicals and other goods.

Reunification and after

After reunification government-owned firms in East Berlin were sold to private owners. But they were old-fashioned and their products did not sell. As a result factories closed and about 155,000 workers lost their jobs. At the same time many West Berliners became unemployed as their businesses no longer received government money and closed down. The situation was made worse by the arrival of East Berliners looking for work.

A new start

Today almost a third of Berlin's industrial workers are employed in electrical engineering. Siemens has the largest workforce in the city. But many more jobs are needed and the Berlin government is trying to attract businesses to the city. The car manufacturer Daimler-Benz and the electrical goods company Sony are both building office and entertainment complexes on Potsdamer Platz in the west. Some firms, such as Coca-Cola, are setting up in the east.

◄ The German car and motorcycle manufacturer BMW has a factory in Spandau, a north-west borough of Berlin.

Crime has risen in Berlin since **reunification**. Yet it is still a reasonably safe city, where the police are always on hand to help.

Berlin police

Berlin, like all other German *Länder*, has its own police force. National forces sometimes also work in the city to deal with major criminals who operate across **Land** borders. Police officers wear a green uniform and drive white and green cars or vans. There are six main police stations in central Berlin. The police station in the Tempelhof borough contains a museum that tells the story of the city's police force.

◄ Berlin's police force drive both cars and vans. They also have a fleet of motorcycles that they use to move quickly through city traffic jams.

The Stasi

Another Berlin museum is devoted to the activities of a more sinister police force. The **Stasi** was East Germany's secret police force and was notorious for spying on its own citizens as well as politicians and visitors from abroad. The Stasi was disbanded in 1989. The Stasi Museum in the organization's former Lichtenberg headquarters contains examples of the bugs and secret cameras that were used.

◄ The Stasi spied on about six million East Germans. In 1991 these people were given the right to see their secret files for the first time.

City crimes

Handbag-snatching in crowded tourist areas is one of the most common crimes in Berlin. The number of violent muggings is also rising, especially in some eastern suburbs, where many people are unemployed and poor. Racist attacks are becoming more frequent (see page 12). Drug-dealing is another serious problem. Sometimes there are also riots and violent demonstrations. For example, students took to the streets in the 1960s, squatters in the 1980s and anti-Gulf War protesters in 1991.

▲ Policemen evict a squatter from a Berlin building. The officers wear riot gear, including helmets that protect their head and neck.

Court system

There are five main types of court in Germany. These include labour courts that deal with employment-related cases, financial courts that deal with tax cases, and of course ordinary courts where criminal trials are held. One of the most famous courts in Berlin is the New Court of Justice in Moabit, part of the Tiergarten borough. This grand 19th-century building has a prison attached where some of Berlin's most notorious criminals spent many unhappy years.

NAZI TERROR

The **Nazi** regime was brutal. Its leaders set up the **Gestapo**, a secret police force, and the **SS** (below), a 'protection squad' that carried out other police duties. Their members imprisoned and tortured anyone who disagreed with Nazi ideas. The headquarters of both organizations was in the Prinz Albrecht Palais in Berlin. The building was later pulled down and underground cells were found. Now an exhibition called the Topography of Terror stands on the site.

GETTING AROUND

As Berlin's industry grew in the 19th century, new forms of transport came to the city. In 1838 the first railway line opened, linking Berlin to Potsdam. Then the U-Bahn (underground) and S-Bahn railway networks were built. Tram and bus services also developed. In 1929 Berlin's transport services became one company, but this collapsed when the city was divided in 1945.

◄ S-Bahn is short for Stadt-Bahn, which means 'city rail'. The S-Bahn network is an ideal way to get around the city and to reach nearby towns such as Potsdam.

Crossing the city

Berlin's transport planners are working to rebuild the transport links from east to west. They have re-opened U-Bahn stations and over 100 km of S-Bahn track that closed after 1945. They are also extending both networks to improve access to the new station (see next page). Many bus routes now run across the city once more. Trams, which from the 1970s ran only in East Berlin, are spreading westwards again too.

Railway renewal

Workers are building a huge railway station in Berlin, near the government complex. When it is completed, as many as 75,000 passengers will catch trains there every day. Underpasses beneath the Tiergarten will give access to the station for both cars and trains. Engineers are also building **maglev trains**, which will run between Berlin and Hamburg in a few years' time. They will travel at up to 500 km per hour.

Cars hurtle along Berlin's famous AVUS ▼ motorway at speeds of up to 100 km/h. The road was originally a motor-racing track.

Cyclists pedal along a ▼ street where part of the Berlin Wall once stood.

WATERWAYS

The Landwehr Canal (left) is part of a network of waterways that extend for about 200 km across Berlin. They connect the River Spree to the Baltic Sea in the north and Poland in the east via other rivers. The canal system is used to carry industrial and other goods to and from Berlin. Goods are loaded and unloaded at the city's 14 harbours, of which the most important is Westhafen. The city authorities intend to increase the use of water transport and are planning a new harbour for the Neukölln borough.

On the road

The Berlin authorities hope that, eventually, 80 per cent of people travelling across the city will use public transport. But at the moment private car traffic is increasing as many Berliners have become car-owners since **reunification**. Their journeys are often unpleasant as all the building work in the city causes frequent traffic jams. The road underpass to the new railway station should help to ease this problem. Many Berliners have found another solution – they travel by bike instead.

Air travel

Berlin has three airports. The major international airports are Tegel in West Berlin and Schönefeld in East Berlin. Tempelhof, in the city centre, is used mainly for flights to and from other German cities. Plans are under way to enlarge Schönefeld Airport to cope with increased air traffic.

SHOPS AND MARKETS

There is plenty to buy in Berlin shops and plenty of time to buy it – on weekdays, most stores stay open until eight o'clock at night. Anyone looking for luxury goods will still find more choice in the west, but smart new shops are gradually opening in the east too.

The Kurfürstendamm, known to ▲ Berliners simply as the Ku'damm, is full of activity all day as well as at night.

▲ Shoppers pause to look at the strange clock in the Europa-Center. The 'fruit juice' flows through the glass tubes and spheres.

Stylish street

Berlin's most famous shopping street is the Kurfürstendamm, in the west. Here, followers of fashion can buy catwalk styles and antique-lovers can call in at the famous Leo Spik auction house. Another highlight of the street is the KPM shop. It sells fine porcelain made by a Berlin company that was set up in 1751 with the help of Frederick the Great.

The Europa-Center

At the eastern end of the Kurfürstendamm is a huge 1960s' shopping complex called the Europa-Center. It is covered in glowing neon advertisements and contains about 100 stores. Inside, there is also a clock full of moving, brightly coloured liquid that Berliners call 'the fruit juice machine' A fountain called The Globe of the World stands outside. Berliners have nicknamed it 'the water dumpling'.

The striking new ➤ Galeries Lafayette store gleams with lights and glass. It was designed by the architect Jean Nouvel.

Top department store

A short way from the Europa-Center is Berlin's most famous shop, KaDeWe. Its name is short for Kaufhaus des Westens, which means 'Department Store of the West'. The store was founded in 1907 and claims to be the biggest in Europe. It sells almost everything, but is especially famous for the food hall on the sixth floor. There shoppers can buy delicacies from all round the world, as well as a huge variety of the great German favourite – sausages (see page 32).

Eastern enterprise

Developers are trying hard to make Friedrichstrasse the East Berlin equivalent of the Kurfürstendamm. Among the new shops is a branch of the Paris department store Galeries Lafayette. Another department store, Quartier 206, is the work of famous Chinese-born American architect IM Pei. It also contains flats, where a few lucky Berliners live. But although these shops are full of high-quality, fashionable goods, they are not yet full of customers.

BERLIN BARGAINS

Open-air markets are a common sight in Berlin. Many sell food, and others are flea markets, where bargains can sometimes be found among the junk. One special market (right) opens every day on Unter den Linden, by the Brandenburg Gate. It is the place to buy Russian fur hats and **Communist** uniforms, as well as supposedly genuine chunks of the Berlin Wall. A completely different but equally fascinating market opens in the borough of Kreuzberg on Tuesday and Friday afternoons. This is the Turkish market, which sells all sorts of Turkish food, including bitter olives, salty cheese and aromatic spices.

FOOD AND DRINK

Many Berliners like to eat heavy, hearty food. Meat, especially pork in the form of chops, sausages, burgers or bacon, features in most meals. But Berlin is a big city, with an international population, so much more is on offer too.

Consumer choice

A wide variety of Berlin restaurants cater for people who do not want to eat traditional food. A few, such as Altes Zollhaus, specialize in a light, modern and expensive style of cooking known as New German Cuisine. The number of vegetarian eating places in the city is growing slowly. They include Zenit, where traditional German dishes are made without meat, and Hakuin, a Buddhist restaurant. Berlin also has many restaurants that specialize in cooking from foreign countries such as Turkey and Italy.

Berlin specialities

Berlin has its own speciality foods. A soup often begins the meal, made for example with liver and dumplings. Main courses include Berlin's best-known dish – knuckle of pork (*Eisbein*). It is usually served with pea purée, sauerkraut and mustard. Other highlights on the menu are pickled pork chops, eel in dill sauce and potato pancakes. A common dessert is red porridge (*Rote Grütze*) – stewed soft fruits, such as raspberries, cherries and blackcurrants – with vanilla sauce.

▲ The well-known Berlin dish of pickled pork chops (*Kassler Rippen*) dates from the reign of Frederick the Great (see page 9).

◄ Grilled sausages (*Bratwürste*) served with tomato ketchup are on the menu at this Berlin street stall.

Café Kranzler once sold ▼ its delicious cakes in East Berlin, but after the **Second World War** the café reopened on the Kurfürstendamm.

BEERS AND BARS

Berlin is a beer-drinker's heaven. The city is full of bars, ranging from *Kneipen* – ordinary, street-corner locals – to themed tourist traps. A large number of cafés also sell beer. There are many types of beer on sale, some of them locally brewed. A speciality of the city is the *Berliner Weisse*, a pale beer made from wheat. Fruit syrup is often added to change the flavour and colour. Raspberry syrup produces a bright red drink, while **woodruff** syrup turns the beer a violent green shade.

Fast food

Fast food is very popular in Berlin. The city's many snack (*Imbiss*) stalls do a roaring trade. They offer a huge range of sausages (*Würste*), including the famous *Currywurst*. This type of sausage, covered in a tomato sauce and curry powder mixture, was invented in Berlin. It was first sold there by a woman called Herta Heuwer in 1948. Other streetside favourites include Doner kebabs, meatballs and chips.

Coffee and cakes

Many Berliners have a sweet tooth. One popular pastime is to spend the afternoon in a café enjoying coffee and cakes (*Kaffee und Kuchen*). Some of the most famous Berlin cafés are old, elegant establishments. The Opern Café on Unter den Linden is in a former palace. The treats on offer in many cafés include apple strudel, Black Forest gâteau and cheesecake, all served with whipped cream. Hot chocolate with cream is a popular alternative to coffee.

ENTERTAINMENT

 Berlin has more than 150 theatres that stage a dazzling range of shows, from serious plays to mainstream musicals and more unusual theatre productions. But **reunification** has caused problems. In particular, lack of money has left some theatres struggling to survive.

▼ The German Theatre opened in 1883. Its magnificent decorations and furnishings were restored as part of the 1983 centenary celebrations.

Serious theatre

In 1948 Bertolt Brecht (see page 41) founded a theatre company in East Berlin. It was called the Berliner Ensemble and it staged his plays at the Theater am Schiffbauerdamm. Now the theatre itself is known as the Berliner Ensemble and still specializes in Brecht's plays. The German Theatre (Deutsches Theater) is the city's oldest and stages both German and non-German classics. Old and new plays are peformed at the Schaubühne am Lehniner Platz.

THE GOLDEN TWENTIES

In the 1920s many Berliners suffered great hardship (see page 10). At the same time a cultural explosion took place in the city. The artistic movement known as **Dadaism** flourished, and Berlin hosted the First International Dada Fair (left). Fritz Lang and other directors made films at the Babelsberg Studios. Painters such as George Grosz, writers such as Bertolt Brecht, and composers such as Arnold Schoenberg created powerful images, words and music that reflected Berlin life. Cabarets and clubs sprang up all over the city where people danced the night away, unaware of the horrors to come.

◄ The Friedrichstadt Palast theatre presents variety shows with singing, dancing and sometimes acrobatics.

Light entertainment

Berlin has four musical theatres, including the famous Theater des Westens, and many cabarets. A popular cabaret is the Bar Jeder Vernunft, a huge tent decorated with mirrors and red velvet. Once the on-stage singing and dancing is over, musicians entertain the audience into the early hours.

Music centre

Berlin is also a centre of classical music. It has two major orchestras. The Berlin Philharmonic Orchestra was established in 1882 and earned great fame under Herbert von Karajan, its conductor from 1955 until 1989. It is housed in a 1960s' building, the Philharmonie in the Kulturforum (see pages 36-37). The Berlin Symphony Orchestra dates from 1952. Its conductor is Vladimir Ashkenazy and it performs in the 19th-century Konzerthaus.

A performance at the Konzerthaus. ▲ The early 19th-century building stands between the French and German Cathedrals on Gendarmenmarkt Square.

Opera houses

Berlin has three opera houses. The oldest, the State Opera House in Unter den Linden, was originally built for Frederick the Great in 1742, and was reconstructed after the **Second World War**. The German Opera in Charlottenburg was built in 1961, after the Berlin Wall cut off West Berliners from the State Opera House. The Comic Opera, also in Unter den Linden, was built in 1947. It specializes in light operas.

Cinema city

Berliners are serious film-goers. The city has about 130 cinemas. The largest is the nine-screen Zoo Palast, but a new 19-screen multiplex and an IMAX cinema are due to open soon in the Daimler-Benz complex on Potsdamer Platz.

MUSEUMS AND ART GALLERIES

Most of Berlin's museums and art galleries are clustered together in four areas of the city: Museum Island (Museuminsel) in the east and the Dahlem, Charlottenburg and Kulturforum complexes in the west. Since **reunification** the Berlin authorities have been reorganizing all four sites to display Berlin's magnificent collections in the best way.

▲ The Bode Museum is named after Wilhelm Bode, manager of Berlin's museums from 1904 to 1920.

Museum Island

Four major museums stand on Museum Island. The Old Museum once contained the Prussian royal family's collection of 1,200 paintings. Now it is a temporary home for 19th-century German art from the Old National Gallery, which is being renovated. Builders are also restoring the island's Bode Museum. This grand building will eventually display a sculpture collection.

The Pergamon Museum

The fourth museum on Museum Island is the Pergamon Museum. It contains valuable objects that German archaeologists brought back from the Middle East and elsewhere in the late 19th and early 20th centuries. Highlights include the Pergamon Altar from Turkey and the Ishtar Gate from Babylon. A fifth museum on the island, the New Museum, was destroyed in the **Second World War**. Reconstruction work is under way.

This section of the marble frieze from ▲ the Pergamon Altar shows a battle scene. It is over 2,000 years old.

The Dahlem Museums

Berlin's museum treasures were stored underground during the war. Afterwards they were divided between East and West Berlin. There was nowhere to display West Berlin's share, so a new museum complex was built in the suburb of Dahlem. One of the most important Dahlem museums is the **Ethnography** Museum. It has eight departments, displaying objects from all over the world.

Charlottenburg

Several galleries and museums can be found in and around Charlottenburg Castle (see page 14). The most important is the Egyptian Museum. Its collection of Egyptian antiquities is among the finest in the world and includes a bust of Queen Nefertiti, wife of the pharaoh Akhenaten, which is about 3,500 years old.

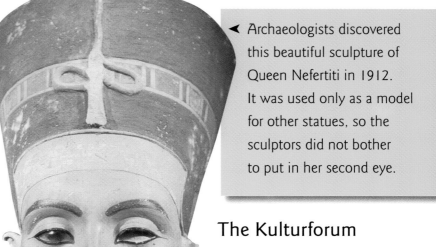

◄ Archaeologists discovered this beautiful sculpture of Queen Nefertiti in 1912. It was used only as a model for other statues, so the sculptors did not bother to put in her second eye.

The Kulturforum

The Kulturforum contains two major art galleries. The Gemäldegalerie has a spectacular collection of paintings that were once divided between the Bode Museum and the Ethnography Museum. It contains works by early European painters including Rembrandt. The New National Gallery displays works by 20th-century artists such as Picasso.

CHECKPOINT CHARLIE

The only official crossing point on the Berlin Wall was nicknamed Checkpoint Charlie. In 1963 the Haus am Checkpoint Charlie Museum opened nearby. Its exhibitions tell the story of the Wall and of the East Berliners who risked – and sometimes lost – their lives fleeing across it. One remaining section of the Wall has become an art exhibition. The 'East Side Gallery' is covered with images such as this (right).

SPECIAL EVENTS

There is always something happening in Berlin. A vast and varied programme of films, music and festivals keeps the city buzzing all year round.

February films

The Berlin International Film Festival brightens up February – about 800 films are shown in just 12 days. A jury chooses the best films at the Zoo Palast cinema. Winners are given gold and silver trophies in the shape of a bear, the symbol of Berlin. In 2000 the focus of the festival will move to the new cinemas on Potsdamer Platz.

Theatre and tennis

A different activity takes over Berlin at the end of April and beginning of May – drama. During the two-week Berlin Drama Festival (Theatertreffen Berlin), German-speaking theatre companies from Austria, Switzerland and Germany perform at various venues. In May Berlin also hosts the German Open Tennis Championships, a top-class contest for women only.

The opening of the Film Festival is ▲ a popular occasion and many people come to catch a glimpse of the stars.

Midsummer music

Berlin vibrates to the sound of music in the summer. The 'Bach Days' take place at the beginning of July in every odd-numbered year. During the nine-day festival, churches, concert halls and palaces host around 30 performances of works by Johann Sebastian Bach, the German composer. The Love Parade, on the second Saturday in July, is a complete contrast. Dance music blares from decorated floats as they make their way through the city. The party often goes on all weekend.

Many people in the Love Parade ➤ enjoy dancing and dressing up. The wilder the outfit, the better!

Autumn highlights

The Berlin Festival Weeks take place in September and each year they celebrate a different country and artistic style. Events are held at venues such as the Konzerthaus and Philharmonie, and include theatre and dance shows, poetry readings and art displays. There is sport to enjoy in the autumn too. About 20,000 runners take part in the Berlin Marathon on the first Sunday in October.

Marathon runners pour through the ➤ Brandenburg Gate. The race ends at the Kaiser William Memorial Church.

◄ Shoppers at this Christmas market in Berlin can enjoy a funfair as well as traditional stalls.

Christmas and New Year

Several Christmas markets open in Berlin during December. The most famous is on the Breitscheidplatz, near the Kaiser William Memorial Church (see page 15). Traditional German items for sale include spiced biscuits and gingerbread. On New Year's Eve some people take part in an organized run through the city. Later on many Berliners celebrate with singing, dancing and fireworks.

GERMAN-AMERICAN FESTIVAL

In 1961, the year the Berlin Wall went up, West Berliners and American forces in their section of the city set up the German-American Festival. The last American troops left Berlin in 1994, but the festival is still going strong. It is held every year in Dahlem from late July to mid-August. Thousands of Berliners go there to enjoy funfair rides, American fast food, gambling and beer.

CITY CHARACTERS

Throughout Berlin's history many great men and women have walked its streets. Here are five of its most famous and influential citizens.

Karl Friedrich Schinkel

Karl Friedrich Schinkel was born in 1781. He trained as an architect in Berlin, and in 1810 began to work for the city's building department. Over the next 20 years Schinkel designed some of Berlin's most impressive buildings, such as the Konzerthaus (see page 35) and the Old Museum (see page 36). Schinkel's influence continued long after his death in 1841. A Schinkel Museum is now open in Berlin's Friedrichwerdersche Church, which he designed.

Ernst Reuter (below ▼ left) at the launch of a radio station. Reuter was the mayor of West Berlin from 1948 until his death in 1953.

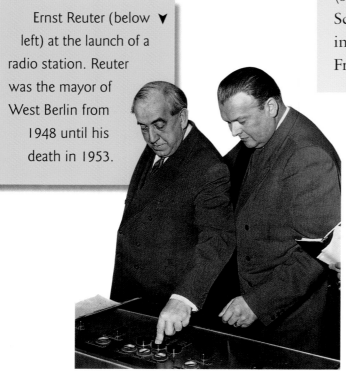

Ernst Reuter

Ernst Reuter was elected Berlin's mayor in 1947. At this time tension was growing between the Soviets and their former allies, and the Soviets did not let Reuter take up the post. Despite this, he worked hard to support Berliners during the airlift (see page 10). Reuter officially became mayor in 1948. He is particularly famous for a speech he made that year. It began: 'Peoples of the world! Look upon this city and admit that you have no right to abandon either the city or the people...'

A square named after Marlene ▲ Dietrich has just opened in Berlin, not far from Potsdamer Platz.

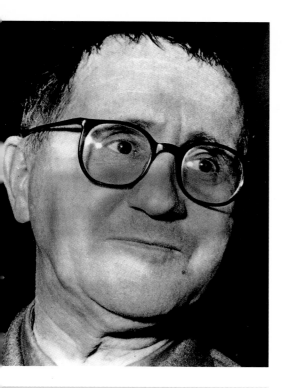

Bertolt Brecht

Bertolt Brecht became a playwright at Berlin's German Theatre in 1924. Four years later his musical drama *The Threepenny Opera* brought him fame. Like many of Brecht's works, it expressed his strong **Marxist** views. Brecht fled abroad in 1933 as the **Nazi** era began. He wrote several plays in this period, including *Mother Courage* (1941). Brecht returned to Berlin in 1948 and founded the Berliner Ensemble (see page 34). He died in 1956.

The Berlin house where Bertolt Brecht ▲ lived is now a museum. It is near the Berliner Ensemble (see page 34), where Brecht worked for many years.

CHRISTA WOLF

Writer Christa Wolf (below) was born in 1929 in a part of Germany that now belongs to Poland. She moved to East Berlin in 1953 and in the 1960s began to publish novels that combine personal and political themes. Wolf's 1963 novel *Divided Heaven*, for example, is both a love story set in Berlin and an expression of **Communist** ideas. Her work also deals with Germany's Nazi past, feminism and the fall of Communism. Wolf's most recent work is a collection of short stories called *Medea* (1996).

Marlene Dietrich

Marlene Dietrich was born in Schöneberg, Berlin, in 1901. In 1922 she made her first stage appearance at the German Theatre, then began to act in films at the Babelsberg Studios. Her big break came when director Josef von Sternberg chose her to star in *The Blue Angel* (1930). She left for Hollywood in 1930, where she built her career. Marlene Dietrich died in 1992. Her body was brought back to Berlin and now lies in Schöneberg's Friedenauer Cemetery.

Change is all around in Berlin. Since **reunification** in 1990, politicians and planners, architects and builders have been working overtime to help the city start afresh. But there is a great deal more to be done.

New arrivals

The most obvious change is the arrival of the **federal** government and parliament in 1999, making Berlin a true capital city once more. Politicians will occupy two parts of the city: the area around the restored Reichstag building and the old government quarter further south. There are also plans to take over part of Museum Island. This would involve building on the site of the **imperial** palace, which was demolished in 1950. Protesters claim that the palace should be reconstructed instead.

▲ English architect Sir Norman Foster planned the restoration of the Reichstag. Its dome had gone (see photograph, page 4), but a new one is now in place.

Berliners in favour of rebuilding the ➤ imperial palace put up a scaffolding framework on the site in 1993. Then they covered it with a huge canvas painted to look like the palace.

Alexanderplatz

Alexanderplatz was the bustling centre of Berlin before the **Second World War**. After the war it was East Berlin's most important square. In the 1960s planners knocked down many of its buildings to create a more '**Communist**' layout. The result is a bleak, grey concrete area surrounded by ugly office blocks and a television tower. Plans are now being made to knock down the square again and build something better.

Local link

Berlin's link with the *Land* of Brandenburg (see page 5) is likely to bring many changes to the city. The aim is to provide greater employment, education and other opportunities for the six million inhabitants of the combined region. Some shared services already exist. But any new joint government will face the hard task of meeting the different needs of people in rural Brandenburg and those in the dynamic new city of Berlin.

EUROPEAN CENTRE

Since the collapse of Communism in Eastern Europe, many former Communist countries, such as Poland and the Czech Republic, have applied to become members of the **European Union**. This eastward expansion could benefit Berlin. Its new position at the heart of the union rather than on its edge should encourage companies to set up new factories and offices there. Berlin also welcomed the introduction of the new European currency, the Euro, on 1 January 1999. The German Euro coins (left) will be issued on 1 January 2002.

Building works

Many other new buildings are planned for Berlin. Some are already under way, including the Daimler-Benz and Sony complexes on Potsdamer Platz (see page 25) and the Jewish Museum in Kreuzberg. There is also a plan for a **Holocaust** memorial to be built near the Brandenburg Gate, on the site of Hitler's Chancellery (see page 14). It will be designed by the American architect Peter Eisenman. A House of Remembrance, where visitors can learn about the Holocaust, will stand nearby.

The new Jewish Museum, in the ▲ Kreuzberg borough, is a stunning silver building. It opened on 24 January 1999.

TIMELINE

This timeline shows some of the most important dates in Berlin's history. All the events are mentioned earlier in this book.

13TH CENTURY

c.1230
St Nicholas Church built
1237
Cölln first mentioned in written records
1244
Berlin first mentioned in written records
c.1270
St Marien Church built

14TH CENTURY

1307
Berlin and Cölln united

17TH CENTURY

1618-1648
Thirty Years' War
1640-1688
Reign of Frederick William, the Great **Elector**
1688
Frederick William is succeeded as Elector of Brandenburg by his son, Frederick

18TH CENTURY

1701
Frederick becomes ruler of **Prussia** and is crowned King Frederick I
French Cathedral completed
1709
Berlin, Cölln and three nearby towns united to form the single city of Berlin
1740
Frederick II (the Great) begins his reign
1791
Brandenburg Gate completed
1793
Peacock Island bought by King Frederick William II

19TH CENTURY

1806-1808
Berlin occupied by French emperor **Napoleon Bonaparte** and his troops
1810
Berlin's oldest university, later known as Humboldt University, founded
1838
First Berlin railway line opened, linking the city to nearby Potsdam
1847
Siemens electrical company set up
1848
Revolution in Berlin
1849
Prussian kings begin to rule with a parliament
1862
New layout prepared for Berlin

1866

New Synagogue completed

1871

German Empire formed and Berlin becomes
the **imperial** capital

1879

Technical University founded

1882

Berlin Philharmonic Orchestra established

1894

Reichstag completed

1895

Kaiser William Memorial Church completed

20TH CENTURY

1905

Berlin Cathedral completed

1914-18

First World War; Germany
is defeated

1918

Kaiser William II **abdicates**

1919

Weimar Republic established

1920

Greater Berlin formed

1929

Berlin's transport services merged

1933

Adolf Hitler becomes German Chancellor

Weimar Republic ended and Third Reich
established

Reichstag damaged by fire

1938

Nazis launch an all-out attack against
Jews on Kristallnacht

Hitler's Chancellery completed

1939

Germany invades Poland

1939-45

Second World War; thousands of Berliners
are killed and many buildings are destroyed
or damaged in air raids

1945

Soviet troops invade Germany, Hitler
commits suicide and Germany surrenders

Germany and Berlin both divided into
four sectors

1948

Free University founded

Berliner Ensemble founded

1948-49

Berlin Airlift takes place

1949

Federal Republic of Germany and
German Democratic Republic formed

1950

Imperial palace demolished

1952

Berlin Symphony Orchestra founded

1961

Berlin Wall erected

1987

St Nicholas Quarter restored as part of
Berlin's 750th anniversary celebrations

1989

Fall of the Berlin Wall

Stasi (East German secret police) disbanded

1990

Berlin and Germany both reunited

1991

Berlin becomes the German capital once
more; politicians vote to move back there

1994

Berlin Banking Company established

Last American troops leave Berlin

1995

Restored New Synagogue opens as museum
and cultural centre

1996

Voters in Berlin and Brandenburg reject
plan to unite their two Länder

1998

German elections take place

1999

German parliament returns to Berlin
and moves into the restored Reichstag

Germany adopts the Euro as its currency

GLOSSARY

abdicated   Gave up (a royal role and title).

air raids   Bombing attacks by enemy aircraft.

Allies   The group of countries that fought against Germany in the Second World War. The four main Allies were Britain, France, the USA and the USSR.

assembly   A group of people who regularly attend meetings to discuss or carry out official business.

Calvinists   People who believe in Protestant Christianity as preached by the 16th-century Swiss religious leader John Calvin.

capitalist   Relating to capitalism, an economic system in which businesses are owned by private individuals rather than the state. *Compare Communist.*

Cold War   The time when the USSR, East Germany and other Communist countries were enemies of the USA, West Germany and other capitalist countries but did not fight them in a violent 'hot' war. The Cold War lasted from about 1945 to 1990.

Communist   Relating to Communism, an economic system in which businesses are owned by the state and there is one political party. *Compare capitalist.*

concentration camps   Large prison camps. The Nazis set up hundreds of concentration camps, where they killed more than six million people, most of them Jews.

constitution   The laws and principles by which a state is governed. Constitutions set out the rights and duties of everyone in society, from ordinary citizens to rulers.

Dadaism   An artistic movement founded in Switzerland in 1915 as a reaction to the horror of the First World War. Its members often created art and literature by jumbling up random images and words.

democracy   A political system in which citizens elect the people who govern them.

Elector   The title given to any German prince who could take part in the election of the Holy Roman Emperor. These emperors ruled much of Europe, including all of Germany, from 800 to 1806.

ethnography   The study of peoples of the world: their ways of life, art, beliefs, and so on.

European Union (EU)   An alliance of 15 European countries, including Germany and the UK. The main aim of the alliance was originally to improve trade, but the member countries now also work together on political matters such as foreign policy.

federal   Relating to a kind of government in which regional and national authorities share power.

First World War   A major war that lasted from 1914 to 1918 and involved a large number of countries. Eventually Germany and Austria-Hungary were defeated by Britain, France, Russia and the USA.

fortifications   Walls or buildings used to defend a city or other area.

Führer   The title used by the Nazi leader Adolf Hitler from 1934 until his death in 1945. It is the German word for leader.

Gestapo   The Nazi secret police force, set up in 1933. The name is short for *Geheime Staatspolizei*, which means secret state police.

Greenwich Mean Time   The time in Greenwich, England, which stands on the zero line of longitude. It is used as a base for calculating the time in the rest of the world.

Holocaust   The murder of millions of Jews and others by the Nazis. Many of the killings took place in concentration camps.

Huguenots   French Protestants, mostly Calvinists.

immigrants   People who come to and settle in a country where they were not born and of which they are not citizens.

imperial   Of or relating to an empire.

inflation   A continual increase in the price of goods.

kindergarten   A school for children who are below the official starting age for education. The word is German for children's garden.

Land   One of the 16 federal states into which Germany is divided. The plural is *Länder*.

maglev trains   Trains that are suspended above tracks and moved along by powerful magnets. The word 'maglev' is short for magnetic levitation.

Marxist   Relating to the ideas of the 19th-century German thinker Karl Marx, who founded Communism.

Napoleon Bonaparte   The gifted general who led France from 1799, ruling as emperor from 1804 until he was defeated in 1815.

Nazi (noun)   A member of the Nazi Party.

Nazi (adjective)   Relating to the Nazi Party.

Nazi Party   The National Socialist German Workers' Party, which was founded in 1919 and led by Adolf Hitler from 1921. The word Nazi is a short form of the German name for the party.

occupied   Took over and ruled.

persecuted   Treated badly; tormented.

pogroms   Organized, violent attacks, especially against Jews.

prefabricated   Ready-made. Tower blocks are often built with concrete blocks made in a factory, and put together on a building site.

Prussia   A large North German state that became a kingdom in 1701 and was abolished after the Second World War.

republic   A country or other political unit with elected rulers and no king or queen.

reunification   Joining as a single unit again; reuniting.

Second World War   A major war that lasted from 1939 to 1945 and involved a large number of countries. Eventually Germany, Italy and Japan were defeated by Britain, France, the USSR and the USA.

Silesia   A European region that was fought over by Prussia and Austria. It is now divided between Poland and the Czech Republic.

Soviet (adjective)   Of or relating to the USSR.

squats   Once empty houses or flats that have been taken over by people who do not pay to live there.

SS   A Nazi organization that was set up in 1925. Its members carried out various duties, for example as concentration camp guards. SS is short for the German word *Schutzstaffel*, which means protection squad.

Stasi   The East German secret police force. The name is short for *Staatssicherheitsdienst*, which means state security service.

state   A country or other political unit that governs itself and makes its own laws.

synagogue   A building where Jews hold their services of worship.

tenement   A large housing block divided into flats.

vocational   Relating to education that trains people for particular careers.

woodruff   A plant with scented leaves that are used to flavour alcohol.

INDEX